HAVE YOU EVER ASKED YOURSELF WHERE?

It's only natural to be confused by the world around us... It is a very complicated and surprising place sometimes! And you'll never understand what's going on around you unless you ask yourself 'WHERE?' every now and again.

'Where' is what this book is all about.

We have travelled over the land, under the sea, up mountains, across deserts – and even into spooky caves – to collect up as many tricky questions as we could find...

...and we also found the answers for you!

We now invite you to come with us on our journey around the world of 'WHERE', so that we can show you all the answers we discovered.

We also thought it might be fun to see how much of this shiny new knowledge you can remember - so at the back of the book, on pages 56 and 57, you'll find some Quick-Quiz questions to test you out. It's not as scary as it sounds - we promise it'll be fun. (And besides, we've given you all the answers on pages 58 and 59.)

While we were searching for all those answers, we found out some other pretty interesting things, too. We wrote them all down on these 'Did you know...' panels - so you can memorize these facts and impress your friends!

Did you know...

The biggest bat colony is in Bracken Cave, Texas, USA. More than 20 million bats roost there.

Are you ready for this big adventure? Then let's go!

WHERE DID THE DINOSAURS GO?

Around 65 million years ago, the dinosaurs vanished. Scientists think Earth was hit by big rocks from outer space, causing dust clouds to block out the Sun. Plants died, then plant-eating dinosaurs and then meat-eaters.

Did you know...

It was not only the dinosaurs that died out 65 million years ago. All the flying reptiles and most of the sea reptiles disappeared, too.

WHERE CAN YOU SEE RIVERS OF ROCK?

Volcanoes are weak spots in the Earth's surface, or crust. Sometimes, a red-hot river of lava pours out of a volcano and flows down its sides. The runny rock can reach temperatures of more than 1,000°C – much, much hotter than an oven – and flow faster than you can run!

Did you know...

Tiger sharks are killing machines even before they are born. Inside their mum's body, the two strongest babies eat up all their brothers and sisters.

Some sharks give birth to live young. Others lay eggs and leave their babies to hatch out on their own. Out in the ocean, baby sharks are at risk from larger predators – including other sharks. Lemon sharks are born in shallow lagoons. They live here in safety for about seven years, hanging around with other young of the same size.

WHERE DO ANGELS, CLOWNS AND PARROTS LIVE?

Did you know...

Some parrotfish coat themselves in mucus at night. These sticky 'pyjamas' seem to make the fish harder for predators to sniff out.

Angelfish, clownfish and parrotfish are just some of the thousands of beautiful animals that live on coral reefs. Reefs grow in shallow water in tropical parts of the world. They contain millions of tiny animals called coral polyps. As each polyp dies, it leaves behind its hard, stony skeleton, building up the reef.

9

WHERE DO I GET MY BALANCE FROM?

Your ears are not just listening machines – they also help you to balance. When you tilt or rotate your head, balance organs in your inner ear send a message to the brain. Then your brain can tell your body how to move so that you do not wobble about.

Did you know...

The smallest bone in your body is in the ear. It is called the stirrup and it is just 2 millimetres long – small enough to sit on top of this letter 'e'.

WHERE DO ELEPHANTS GLOW IN THE DARK?

For the Sri Lankan festival of the Esala Perahera, people dress elephants in beautiful costumes and decorate them with strings of electric lights. There is a night-time procession of more than 50 elephants, along with thousands of drummers and dancers.

Did you know...

The Esala Perahera is a Buddhist festival. The elephants carry a holy relic – believed to be the tooth of the Buddha himself – through the streets.

WHERE DO BEARS GO IN WINTER?

Did you know...

The Alaskan grizzly is the largest kind of brown bear. A male standing on all fours is 1.5 metres tall.

Black and brown bears live in the cold forests of the far north. They escape the winter chill by snuggling up in their den, which might be in a cave or a hollow tree. They sleep most of the time, living off the body fat they stored up during the summer.

WHERE IS THE WORLD OF THE ICE GIANTS?

Did you know...

The World of the Ice Giants was discovered in 1879 and opened to the public in 1912. In places, the ice is 20 metres thick.

You will have to take a trip to Austria to visit the World of the Ice Giants, or Eisriesenwelt, the world's biggest system of ice caves. Ice caves form inside solid rock, as a cave's rock walls become coated in ice that stays frozen all year round.

WHERE IS IT NIGHT ALL DAY LONG?

Did you know...

In summer, it is all change at the poles. The Sun is in the sky morning, noon and night. On midsummer's night, the Sun never goes down and people hold big parties.

During the winter months, the lands around the poles do not see the Sun at all. The Sun is so low in the sky that it is hidden below the horizon. This makes the days cold and dark – even at midday. In Scandinavia, in northern Europe, children go to and from school by the light of the Moon or stars.

14

WHERE MIGHT YOU FIND A PHARAOH?

Did you know...

Many pharaohs were buried in desert tombs in a place called the Valley of the Kings. The most famous tomb was for the boy king, Tutankhamun.

The ancient Egyptians called their kings pharaohs. When a pharaoh died, they dried out his body and preserved it as a mummy. Today, you can see mummified pharaohs in museums, but some pharaohs are still hidden in their desert tombs.

WHERE ARE THE PYRAMIDS?

The pyramids were huge tombs for dead pharaohs. There are pyramids at more than 80 sites in Egypt, but the most famous three are at Giza on the bank of the River Nile. They were built more than 4,500 years ago for the pharaohs Khufu, Khafra and Menkaura.

Did you know...

A huge statue of a sphinx guards the pyramids at Giza. It has a lion's body and a human head. The statue is vast – more than 70 metres long and 20 metres high.

WHERE DO RAINBOWS HAPPEN?

You can see a rainbow when there are water droplets in the air, such as in mist or rain, and when the Sun is behind you and at a low angle. Sunlight is actually made up of lots of colours. When it shines through the water droplets, the light splits into all of these colours.

WHERE DOES IT RAIN FOR A MONTH?

Did you know...

Mawsynram in India is the wettest place on Earth. An average of 11,870 millimetres of rain falls there every year, most of it in the monsoon season.

Many tropical countries have a dry season and a wet season. Some parts of India and Southeast Asia have long, heavy downpours called monsoons. Big, black clouds blow in from the sea during the summer months. Once the rain starts, it can last for weeks, flooding the fields and the streets.

WHERE DOES CHOCOLATE GROW ON TREES?

Did you know...

The Maya people were drinking hot chocolate more than 1,500 years ago. They preferred it bitter, not sweet, and one favourite flavouring was spicy chilli!

Chocolate is made from the seeds of the cacao tree. Sadly, this tree does not grow everywhere - just in hot, wet places. The cacao tree originated in Central and South America. Today, it also grows on plantations in Southeast Asia and West Africa.

WHERE DO PLANTS GROW?

There are about 380,000 different kinds of plant on Earth, and they grow just about everywhere – in fields and forests, deserts and mountains, rivers and lakes. Apart from air, the two things plants need are sunlight and water, so they cannot grow in places that are completely dark or dry.

WHERE DOES MY FOOD GO?

Did you know...

Your small intestine, where the nutrients in your food pass into your body, is an amazing 6 metres long!

When you swallow food, it passes down your throat into your stomach, where it is mashed into a kind of soup. This 'soup' is squeezed along a winding tube called your intestine. By now, the useful bits of food are tiny enough to be taken into your blood and carried around your body, to give it energy to live and grow.

WHERE DOES COAL COME FROM?

Did you know...

The period from 355 to 290 million years ago is known as the age of coal. Some amazing plants grew during this time, including gigantic clubmosses that towered 40 metres high.

Most of the coal we burn today was formed from the fossilized remains of prehistoric forests that covered the land between 355 and 290 million years ago. Layers of plant matter built up on the beds of shallow seas. Over millions of years, the plant matter was pressed down and transformed into layers of hard, black rock.

WHERE CAN I SAVE ENERGY?

We use energy all the time - it powers our cars and lights and heats our homes. One way to save energy is to walk or cycle to school instead of going by car. Other ways include turning off the light when you leave a room, and keeping heat from escaping using insulation or a 'draught excluder' (below). You can also replace any old-style light bulbs in your home with energy-saving bulbs (below, left) instead.

WHERE DOES UNDERWATER GRASS GROW?

Did you know...

Despite their plant-like appearance, seaweeds are not plants. They belong to a different group of living things, called algae.

Seagrass grows in shallow water and is the only ocean plant that has flowers. Its leaves are long and green, like blades of grass. Seagrass often forms underwater 'meadows', where dugongs come to graze. Dugongs are also known as sea cows.

WHERE IS THE BIGGEST ANIMAL?

Did you know...

The largest land animal is the African elephant. An adult male weighs around 7 tonnes – the same as seven family cars.

The blue whale is the biggest animal ever to have lived on Earth, and it lives in the world's oceans. It is so long that eight elephants could stand along its back, and so heavy that it weighs as much as 150 cars! On land, an animal as big as the blue whale would collapse under its own weight. In the ocean, the water supports its body better.

WHERE DOES THE BIGGEST REPTILE LIVE?

Did you know...

In short bursts, a saltwater crocodile can zip through the water at speeds of up to 8 metres per second.

The biggest living reptile is the saltwater crocodile of tropical Asia and Australia. As its name suggests, it is at home in salt water and may swim far out to sea. During the wet season, though, it spends its time inland in freshwater rivers and swamps. The 'saltie' lurks near the water's edge, waiting for unsuspecting prey to come near.

Did you know...

Hippos used to be common all along the Nile. They are the second-largest land animals, after the elephant. Hippo males are as long as a car!

The world's longest river is the Nile, which flows up through North Africa. It is about 6,650 kilometres long – 250 kilometres longer than the Amazon river in South America.

WHERE DO ANGELS FALL?

Did you know...

The Venezuelan name for the falls is Kerepakupai Merú, which means 'waterfall of the deepest place' in a local language.

Angel Falls in Venezuela, South America, is the world's tallest waterfall, measuring 979 metres. The wind blows much of the water into mist. The falls are named after an American adventurer, James Angel, who crashed his plane nearby in the 1930s.

WHERE DOES THE SUN GO AT NIGHT?

Over the course of a day, the Sun seems to travel across the sky, from east to west, then sink below the horizon. The Sun has gone and it is night! This happens because the Earth is turning all the time. While your half of the planet is turned away from the Sun, experiencing night, the opposite half of the world is facing the Sun, experiencing its daytime.

Did you know...

The ancient Greeks believed that the Sun was a god, riding across the sky in his blazing chariot.

WHERE DO KOALAS LIVE?

Did you know...

Koalas get water from their food and rarely need to drink. Their name comes from an Australian Aboriginal word meaning 'no drink'.

Koalas are picky creatures. They eat only the leaves and young shoots of eucalyptus trees. So the only place koalas live, in the wild, is in the eucalyptus forests of Australia.

WHERE IS THERE LAND BUT NO COUNTRIES?

Did you know...

No one lives in Antarctica except for a few hundred scientists. They study rocks, the weather, and plant and animal life.

The vast, frozen land around the South Pole is called Antarctica. It is not a country because it has no people, no government and no flag. Many countries have signed an agreement, promising to keep Antarctica as a wilderness where scientists from all nations can study.

WHERE WAS THE HEAVIEST SNOWFALL?

38

Did you know...

The largest single snowstorm on record was in Alaska, USA, in 1955. It lasted for 5 days and dumped nearly 4,450 millimetres of snow.

In the 12-month period from 19 February 1971 to 18 February 1972, an amazing 31,102 millimetres of snow fell on Mount Rainier, in the USA. That is about the same depth of snow as 19 people standing on each other's heads!

WHERE DID BIRDS COME FROM?

Dinosaurs may not have been able to fly, but scientists agree that birds evolved from small, feathered dinosaurs called maniraptorans. The oldest known dino-bird was Archaeopteryx, which lived 150 million years ago in the Jurassic Period. It had large hand claws and a toothed jaw.

WHERE ARE DINOSAUR FOSSILS FOUND?

Dinosaurs lived all over the Earth. Their fossils have been found in places as far apart as the USA and China, England and Australia – even in Antarctica. Fossils are usually buried inside rock, so they have to be dug out.

WHERE ARE THE HIGHEST MOUNTAINS?

Did you know...

The longest mountain range on land is the Andes, in South America. It is about 7,200 kilometres long – nearly three times longer than the Himalayas.

The world's highest mountains are the Himalayas of central Asia. The mountain range has more than 110 snow-covered peaks, including Mount Everest – the world's tallest mountain – which rises to about 8,850 metres. Only the toughest plants and hardiest animals can survive the extreme conditions up here.

WHERE DOES THE WIND GET WINDIEST?

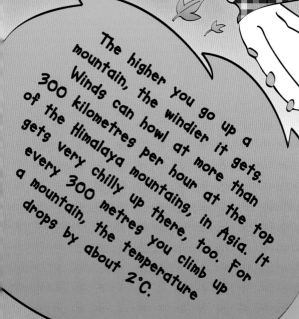

The higher you go up a mountain, the windier it gets. Winds can howl at more than 300 kilometres per hour at the top of the Himalaya mountains, in Asia. It gets very chilly up there, too. For every 300 metres you climb up a mountain, the temperature drops by about 2°C.

WHERE DOES IT NEVER RAIN?

Did you know...

The Atacama desert in Chile, South America, is the world's driest desert. It had no rain for 400 years. Then, in 1971, it suddenly poured!

Deserts are the world's driest places because they never – or hardly ever – have rain. Some deserts are hot and sandy. Others are cold regions with frozen soil.

WHERE WOULD YOU FIND A RUNNING PLANT?

The bird-cage plant lives in the deserts of the American West. It puts down shallow roots in the shade of a dune to suck up what little water there is. If the sand shifts, the plant may find itself in scorching sunlight. So it leaves behind its shrivelled roots and speeds off across the sand to find a new place to live. It has no legs, but its cage-like, round body allows it to roll along like a ball.

Did you know...

In many desert plants, the above-ground part breaks away and moves off to scatter seeds. They are known as tumbleweeds.

WHERE WERE THE FIRST OLYMPICS?

Did you know...

Only men could compete in the ancient Olympics. Women had their own games, in honour of Hera, the queen of the gods. There was just one event – running.

The first Olympic Games were held in ancient Greece as part of a festival to honour Zeus, the king of the gods. Every four years, thousands of spectators flocked to Olympia to see athletes run, box, wrestle and race chariots (speedy, horse-drawn carts).

43

WHERE IS THE EYE OF A HURRICANE?

Did you know...

In the Far East, hurricanes are called typhoons. In India and Australia, they are known as cyclones.

With winds roaring at more than 117 kilometres per hour, hurricanes are the fiercest storms on Earth. At their centre, though, is the eye – an area where the wind is fairly calm and there are no big storm clouds. The fast and furious hurricane winds move in a spiral around the eye.

WHERE DO EARTHQUAKES HAPPEN?

Did you know...

In Japanese legends, a giant catfish called Namazu triggers earthquakes by wriggling about.

Earthquakes make the ground shake. The most violent ones can move mountains, make rivers change course and bring cities tumbling to the ground. Like volcanoes, earthquakes happen at weak spots on the Earth's surface, where two plates - massive sections of land - bump or grind together.

WHERE WOULD YOU FIND A FLYING WEAVER?

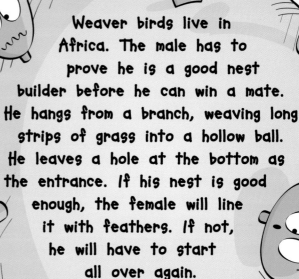

Weaver birds live in Africa. The male has to prove he is a good nest builder before he can win a mate. He hangs from a branch, weaving long strips of grass into a hollow ball. He leaves a hole at the bottom as the entrance. If his nest is good enough, the female will line it with feathers. If not, he will have to start all over again.

WHERE DO BIRDS LIVE IN CITIES?

Did you know...

Mockingbirds on the Galápagos Islands snatch hair from people's heads to line their nests. A cheap – but rather painful – haircut!

For many seabirds, a cliff is the perfect place to nest – safe from hunters and handy for fishing. Thousands of birds lay their eggs on the narrow ledges or nest in cracks in the rocks. With all those birds fighting for space, the cliff is like a city – crowded, smelly and very noisy!

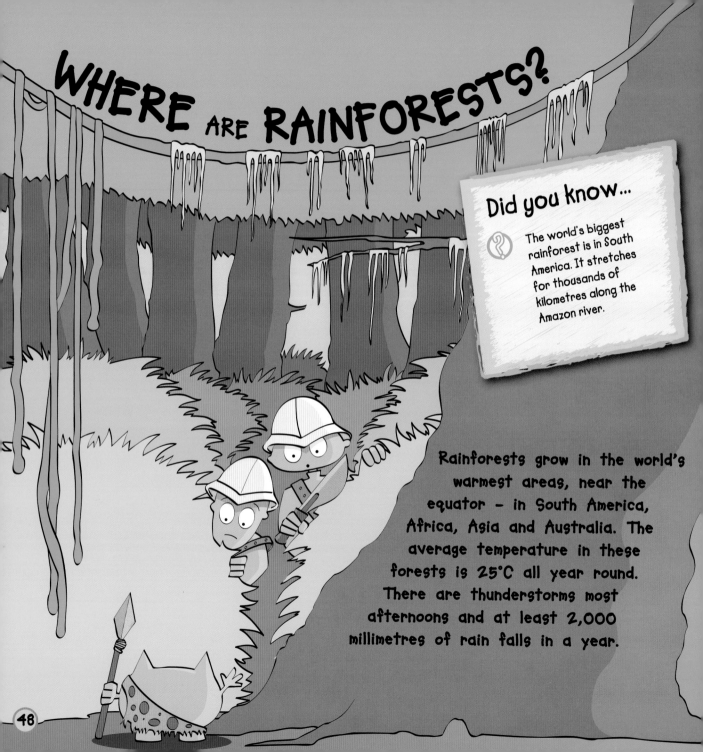

WHERE ARE RAINFORESTS?

Did you know...

The world's biggest rainforest is in South America. It stretches for thousands of kilometres along the Amazon river.

Rainforests grow in the world's warmest areas, near the equator – in South America, Africa, Asia and Australia. The average temperature in these forests is 25°C all year round. There are thunderstorms most afternoons and at least 2,000 millimetres of rain falls in a year.

Did you know...

This book started life as a tree trunk. Most paper comes from coniferous trees, such as spruce and pine.

The world's biggest forest is called the boreal forest. 'Boreal' means 'northern', and this forest stretches right the way across northern Europe and Asia. All its trees are conifers – they have hard, narrow leaves called needles to withstand the cold. The boreal forest is home to brown bears, wolves and reindeer.

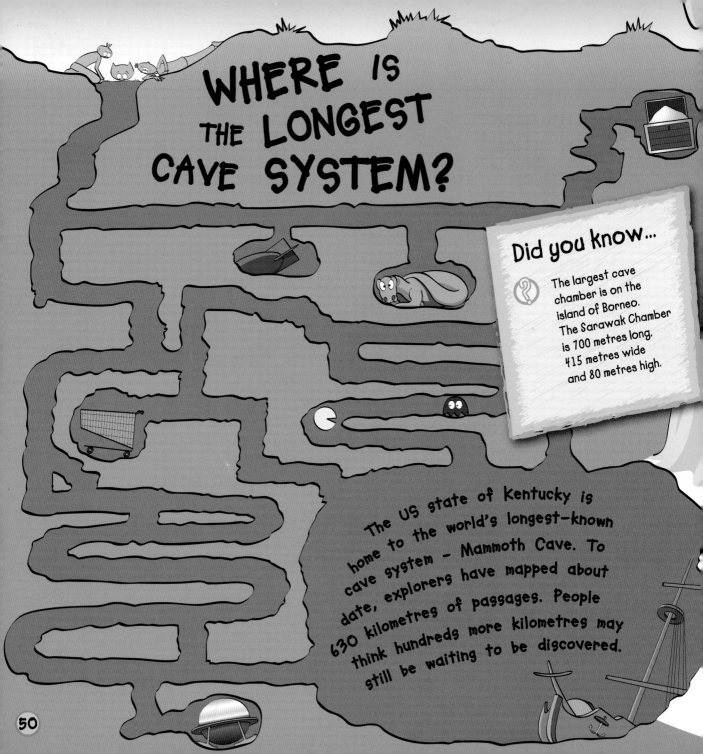

WHERE IS THE LONGEST CAVE SYSTEM?

Did you know...

The largest cave chamber is on the island of Borneo. The Sarawak Chamber is 700 metres long, 415 metres wide and 80 metres high.

The US state of Kentucky is home to the world's longest-known cave system – Mammoth Cave. To date, explorers have mapped about 630 kilometres of passages. People think hundreds more kilometres may still be waiting to be discovered.

WHERE CAN YOU PLAY SPORT IN A CAVE?

Norway's Gjøvik Rock Cavern was blasted from the rock to house a huge, underground sports stadium where ice hockey matches were held during the 1994 Winter Olympics. At 91 metres long and 61 metres wide, it is one of the world's largest artificial rock chambers.

Did you know...

Not all farmers grow their crops in fields. Some use caves instead! The cool, dark conditions of a cave are perfect for growing mushrooms.

WHERE DO WOMEN WEAR BOWLER HATS?

Did you know...

Bowler hats were first made for men, not women. British businessmen have worn them to work for more than 160 years.

In the Andes mountains of South America, many of the women wear round bowler hats. The hat has become a part of their traditional dress, along with a full skirt and a colourful poncho (warm cloak) made of llama wool.

52

WHERE DO MEN WEAR SKIRTS?

Did you know...

In Scotland, each clan (family group) has its own kinds of tartan, each with a particular pattern and set of colours.

On special occasions, it is traditional for Scottish men to wear kilts. Kilts are pleated skirts made from a checked, woollen cloth called tartan. They are warm, but they only come down to the knee, so they are worn with a pair of long, woolly socks.

WHERE DID CHINA COME FROM?

Did you know...

Porcelain is 'fired' (heated fiercely) in an extremely hot kiln oven, where the temperature reaches up to 1,200°C. Phew!

Although pottery was made all over the world from early times, the very finest kind, porcelain, was invented in southern China in around 600CE. This is why we often refer to it as 'china'!

WHERE DOES IT TAKE HOURS TO DRINK TEA?

Did you know...

The biggest-ever tea party was held in Australia, in 2005, at various places across the country. More than 280,000 people took part.

In Japan, there is a special, ancient tea ceremony called chanoyu. The tea is made so slowly, and sipped so carefully, that it really does take hours. It is not a good idea to turn up to the ceremony feeling thirsty!

QUICK-QUIZ QUESTIONS

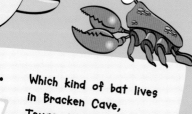

7. Which kind of bat lives in Bracken Cave, Texas, USA?

1. When did the dinosaurs disappear?

2. Vulcanologists study aliens. True or false?

8. Unscramble MAN TUTU HANK to find the name of a famous young pharaoh.

9. In what order do the seven colours of the rainbow appear?

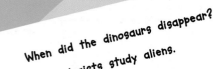

3. Unscramble SIP FOR HART to find a coral reef fish.

4. Where is the smallest bone in the human body?

10. How much rain falls each year in the world's wettest place?

5. The Hindu festival of Esala Perahera features lit-up rhinos. True or false?

6. What is another name for the 'Eisriesenwelt'?

11. How many different kinds of plant are there?

12. Unscramble CENT IN DANCES to find a kind of light bulb.

13. Seaweed is a plant. True or false?

14. How long is the Great Barrier Reef?

15. Which is the world's second-longest river?

16. What do koalas eat?

17. Unscramble OY RAT CAPER HEX to find the name of one of the first birds.

18. How tall is the highest mountain on Earth?

19. Which desert had no rain for 400 years?

20. Who were the king and queen of the Greek gods?

21. What is the name of the earthquake-causing catfish in Japanese mythology?

22. Which continent is home to the largest rainforest?

23. Python Cave is the world's longest cave system. True or false?

24. Which country hosted the 1994 Winter Olympics?

25. What would you be served at a chanoyu?

QUICK-QUIZ
ANSWERS

1. About 65 million years ago.

2. False. They study volcanoes.

7. The Mexican free-tailed bat.

3. SIP FOR HART = Parrotfish.

8. MAN TUTU HANK = Tutankhamun.

4. Inside the ear.

9. Red, orange, yellow, green, blue, indigo, violet.

5. False. Esala Perahera is a Buddhist festival, and the animals on parade are elephants.

10. An average of 11,870 millimetres.

11. About 380,000.

6. The World of the Ice Giants.

12. CENT IN DANCES = Incandescent.

13. False. Seaweed is an alga, not a plant.

14. More than 2,000 kilometres long.

15. The Amazon.

16. Eucalyptus leaves and shoots.

17. OY RAT CAPER HEX = Archaeopteryx.

18. About 8,850 metres tall.

19. The Atacama desert, in Chile.

20. Zeus and Hera.

21. Namazu.

22. South America (the Amazon rainforest).

23. False. Mammoth Cave is the longest cave system.

24. Norway.

25. Tea.

TRICKY WORDS

ALGAE
'Algae' is the overall name for a group of very simple living things. Seaweeds are algae.

ANCIENT EGYPTIANS
People who lived in Egypt, from around 5,000 to 2,000 years ago.

ANCIENT GREEKS
People who lived in and around Greece, from around 3,000 to 1,600 years ago.

ANTARCTICA
Earth's icy, southernmost area around the South Pole.

CONTINENT
One of the Earth's seven main landmasses - North America, South America, Europe, Africa, Asia, Australia and Antarctica.

DESERT
A dry region with little plant life.

DINO-BIRD
An animal that shares characteristics of dinosaurs and modern birds. Birds evolved from dinosaurs hundreds of millions of years ago.

DUGONG
A plant-eating sea mammal found in shallow, warm waters of the Indian and Pacific oceans.

EARTH'S CRUST
The outer layer of planet Earth, on which we live.

EQUATOR
The imaginary line that circles the middle of the Earth.

EVOLVE
To change from one species to another over millions of years, by passing on useful characteristics from one generation to the next.

FOSSIL
The remains of a plant or creature that existed long ago. Fossils are usually formed from the hard parts of an animal or plant, such as teeth, bones or shells. They are created when, for example, animal bones sink into mud, which then gradually hardens into rock.

HORIZON
The line, in the distance, at which the Earth's surface and the sky appear to meet.

HURRICANE
A strong storm that forms over warm seas. Its winds can travel at more than 117 kilometres per hour.

INCANDESCENT LIGHT BULB
A light bulb that creates light by heating a thin, metal wire - called a filament - so that it glows. The filament is protected inside a glass bulb.

INVENTOR
A person who is the first to think of or create something, such as a machine.

LAGOON
A pool of salt water that is separated from the sea, for example by a reef.

LAVA
Liquid rock that spurts from volcanoes or cracks in the Earth's crust (surface layer).

LEGEND
A story that has been told for a long time.

MAYA
Ancient people who lived in Mexico and northern Central America, from around 3,500 to 1,000 years ago.

MONSOON
The rainy season in India and Southeast Asia. A seasonal wind, also called the monsoon, brings the rains.

MUCUS
A slimy substance squeezed out by an animal's glands.

OLYMPIC GAMES
International sporting events that take place every four years. The first Games were held in ancient Greece.

PLANTATION
A large farm where just one crop - for example cacao, coffee or tea - is grown for money.

PREDATOR
An animal that hunts and eats another animal.

PREHISTORIC
Describes the period of history before our written records began.

PREY
An animal that is hunted and eaten by another animal.

PYRAMID
A large, stone building with four triangular sides. The ancient Egyptians built pyramids as tombs.

REEF
A long line of rock, sand or coral that lies just beneath the surface of the sea.

REPTILE
An animal with a backbone and scaly skin. Most reptiles lay eggs on land, but some give birth to live young.

ROMANS
Ancient people from Italy who lived around 2,000 years ago in Europe, Africa and Asia.

SHALE
Fine rock formed from hardened mud and clay.

SPHINX
An ancient Egyptian statue with a lion's body and a human or animal head.

TARTAN
A woven cloth from Scotland, made from wool and patterned with checks and stripes of different thicknesses and colours.

VOLCANO
A vent (hole) in the surface or crust of a planet through which gas, ash and molten rock escape. The material that erupts can build up to form a mountain.

VULCANOLOGIST
Someone whose job it is to study volcanoes.

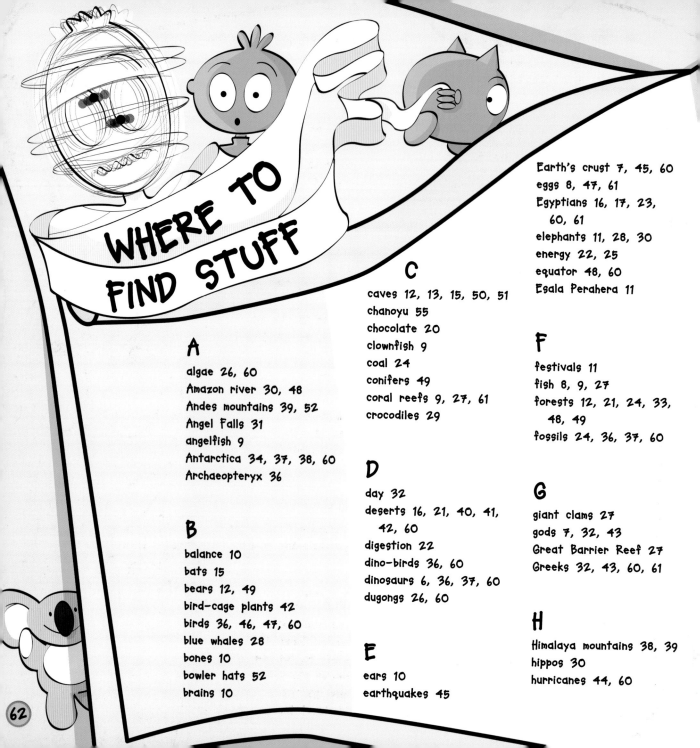

WHERE TO FIND STUFF

Wow! What an amazing journey! We hope you had as much fun as we did, and learnt many new things. Who knew there was so much to discover about 'where'! Here are some other exciting books 'where' you'll find more to explore:

The Book Of... How?
The Book Of... What?
The Book Of... Which?
The Book Of... Who?
The Book Of... Why?

Look out for these great books! 'Who' knows 'what' we'll discover...

See you soon!